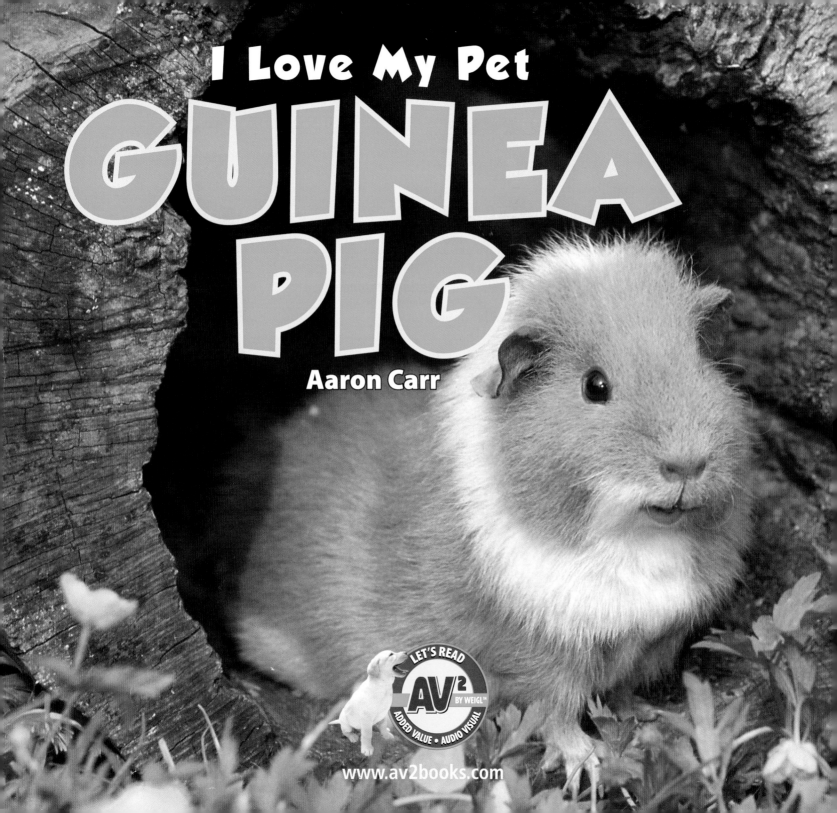

I Love My Pet

GUINEA PIG

Aaron Carr

LET'S READ
AV²
BY WEIGL™
ADDED VALUE • AUDIO VISUAL

Go to **www.av2books.com,** and enter this book's unique code.

BOOK CODE

J897768

AV² by Weigl brings you media enhanced books that support active learning.

AV² provides enriched content that supplements and complements this book. Weigl's AV² books strive to create inspired learning and engage young minds in a total learning experience.

Your AV² Media Enhanced books come alive with...

Audio
Listen to sections of the book read aloud.

Key Words
Study vocabulary, and complete a matching word activity.

Video
Watch informative video clips.

Quizzes
Test your knowledge.

Embedded Weblinks
Gain additional information for research.

Slide Show
View images and captions, and prepare a presentation.

Try This!
Complete activities and hands-on experiments.

... and much, much more!

Published by AV² by Weigl
350 5th Avenue, 59th Floor New York, NY 10118
Website: www.av2books.com www.weigl.com

W 23.99 May 2/14

Library of Congress Cataloguing in Publication data available upon request.
Fax 1-866-449-3445 for the attention of the Publishing Records department.

ISBN 978-1-62127-294-6 (hardcover)
ISBN 978-1-62127-300-4 (softcover)

Printed in the United States of America in North Mankato, Minnesota
1 2 3 4 5 6 7 8 9 0   16 15 14 13 12

122012
WEP301112

Senior Editor: Aaron Carr   Art Director: Terry Paulhus

Weigl acknowledges Getty Images as the primary image supplier for this title. Cover: Livia Unger.

I Love My Pet
GUINEA PIG

CONTENTS

3

I love my pet guinea pig.
I take good care of him.

My pet guinea pig
was three weeks old
when I brought him home.
He was called a puppy
when he was a baby.

My pet guinea pig was full grown after five months. He weighs about 2 pounds.

Guinea pigs can grow up to 16 inches long.

10

My pet guinea pig has teeth
that never stop growing.
He chews on things to keep
his teeth from getting too long.

My pet guinea pig
has three toes on his back feet
and four toes on his front feet.

Guinea pigs have
sharp claws on
their toes.

13

My pet guinea pig
uses his teeth and claws
to brush his fur.
I help brush him once a week.

My pet guinea pig eats fruits and vegetables. He has to be fed fresh food every day.

My pet guinea pig
gets scared very easily.
He does not like loud noises.

I make sure
my pet guinea pig is healthy.
I love my pet guinea pig.

GUINEA PIG FACTS

These pages provide more detail about the interesting facts found in the book. They are intended to be used by adults as a learning support to help young readers round out their knowledge of each animal featured in the *I Love My Pet* series.

Pages 4–5

I love my pet guinea pig. I take good care of him. The guinea pig is a type of rodent, similar to hamsters, chinchillas, and mice. Guinea pigs make good pets. They are small and gentle animals that are easy to care for. They are clean, quiet, and do not take up much space. Still, guinea pigs need care and attention every day.

Pages 6–7

My pet guinea pig was three weeks old when I brought him home. He was called a puppy when he was a baby. Unlike hamsters and rabbits, guinea pig puppies are born with fur, open eyes, and teeth. They are able to walk a few days after birth. By three to five weeks of age, guinea pig puppies stop drinking their mother's milk. They are now able to live on their own.

Pages 8–9

My pet guinea pig was full-grown after five months. He weighs about 2 pounds. A full-grown guinea pig can range in size from 7 to 16 inches (20 to 40 centimeters) in length and weigh between 1 and 3 pounds (0.5 and 1.5 kg). A male guinea pig is called a boar. A female is called a sow.

Pages 10–11

My pet guinea pig has teeth that never stop growing. He chews on things to keep his teeth from getting too long. Guinea pigs have 20 teeth. Their teeth are open rooted, which means they grow continuously. To keep their teeth from growing too long, guinea pigs must have something to chew on, such as a piece of wood. Teeth that have grown too long can cause health problems.

Pages 12–13

My pet guinea pig has three toes on his back feet and four toes on his front feet. Each of a guinea pig's 14 toes has a short, sharp claw. The bottoms of the guinea pig's feet are covered by a soft, leathery pad. The pads help protect the guinea pig's tiny toe bones. Guinea pigs have fragile bones, so they must always be handled with care.

Pages 14–15

My pet guinea pig uses his teeth and claws to brush his fur. I help brush him once a week. Guinea pigs like to be well groomed. Although guinea pigs will groom themselves, they also need help from their owners. A toothbrush makes a perfect guinea pig brush. Long-haired guinea pigs need to be brushed more often.

Pages 16–17

My pet guinea pig eats fruits and vegetables. He has to be fed fresh food every day. Guinea pigs are herbivores. This means they only eat plants, such as fruits, vegetables, and grains. Guinea pigs need to be fed twice a day, with meals around the same time each day. To ensure guinea pigs get the nutrients they need, feed them special guinea pig feed pellets with a mixture of fresh food.

Pages 18–19

My pet guinea pig gets scared very easily. He does not like loud noises. Guinea pigs have very sensitive ears. They can hear high-pitched sounds better than humans. Loud or high-pitched noises can scare guinea pigs or hurt their ears. A guinea pig's cage should be placed in a quiet spot away from loud noises. It is also good to speak softly when handling your pet.

Pages 20–21

I make sure my pet guinea pig is healthy. I love my pet guinea pig. Properly cared for guinea pigs will usually stay healthy and happy. It is rare for a guinea pig to become sick. Keep handling to a minimum. If your guinea pig starts to eat or exercise less, or if there is wetness around his eyes and nose, take him to a veterinarian right away.

KEY WORDS

Research has shown that as much as 65 percent of all written material published in English is made up of 300 words. These 300 words cannot be taught using pictures or learned by sounding them out. They must be recognized by sight. This book contains 52 common sight words to help young readers improve their reading fluency and comprehension. This book also teaches young readers several important content words, such as proper nouns. These words are paired with pictures to aid in learning and improve understanding.

Page	Sight Words First Appearance
4	good, him, I, my, of, take
7	a, called, he, home, old, three, was, when
9	about, after, can, grown, long, to, up
11	from, has, his, keep, never, on, stop, that, things, too
12	and, back, feet, four, have, their
15	help, once, uses
17	be, day, eats, every, food
18	does, gets, like, not, very
21	is, make

Page	Content Words First Appearance
4	guinea pig, pet
7	baby, puppy, weeks
9	inches, months, pounds
11	teeth
12	claws, front, toes
15	fur
17	fruits, vegetables
18	noises, scared
21	healthy

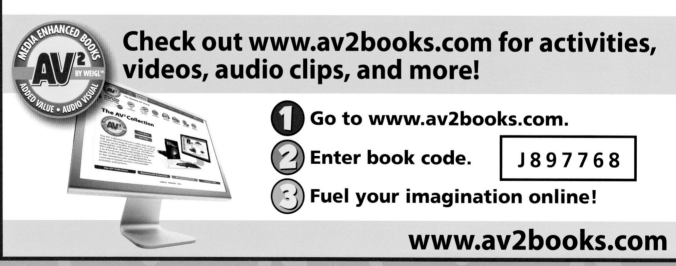